AF891909

Fair Housing Haiku

5

Learn About the Law Through Verse

7

With Illustrations

5

Fair Housing Haiku[5]

Learn About the Law Through Verse[7]

With Illustrations[5]

Written and Illustrated by

Ron Leshnower

Hillocrian Creative

FAIR HOUSING HAIKU: LEARN ABOUT THE LAW THROUGH VERSE / WITH ILLUSTRATIONS
RON LESHNOWER

Copyright © 2018 Ron Leshnower

All rights reserved. Except as permitted by law, no part of this publication may be reproduced, distributed, or transmitted in any form or by any means, or stored in a database or retrieval system, without the prior written permission of the publisher and author.

Hillocrian Creative LLC
P.O. Box 1248
Melville, NY 11747
www.hillocriancreative.com
info@hillocriancreative.com

ISBN-10: 0-9892911-5-4 ISBN-13: 978-0-9892911-5-6

Printed in the United States of America

Cover and book design by Ron Leshnower

Equal housing opportunity logo courtesy of the U.S. Department of Housing and Urban Development.

First Edition: April 2018

10 9 8 7 6 5 4 3 2 1

Visit WWW.FAIRHOUSINGHAIKU.COM for more information.

Limit of Liability/Disclaimer of Warranty: While the publisher and author have used their best efforts in preparing this book, they make no representations or warranties with respect to the accuracy or completeness of its contents and specifically disclaim any implied warranties or merchantability or fitness for a particular purpose. Neither the publisher nor author shall be liable for any loss or profit or any other commercial damages, including but not limited to special, incidental, consequential, or other damages.

Legal Disclaimer: This book is designed to provide accurate information in regard to the subject matter covered. It is sold with the understanding that the author and publisher are not engaged in rendering legal advice or other professional services. If legal advice is required, the services of a competent attorney should be sought.

For more information about Hillocrian Creative products, visit www.hillocriancreative.com and follow @hillocrian on Twitter.

Also, follow @fairhousing for housing discrimination news and developments.

For Jacob the text,
and the illustrations for
Chloe, with my love.

For Hillary too—
Hillocrian Creative
was inspired by you.

Table of Contents

Preface (to explain why this book was written and what it's all about)

Fifty years ago,
the Fair Housing Act became
the law of the land.

50
FAIR HOUSING ACT

EST. 1968

This book was written
for this anniversary,
to help spread knowledge

of how fair housing—
against all odds—became part
of America.

For a new approach,
this book was penned in haiku—
in 5-7-5—

with illustrations
(such as the one you see here)
to support the text.

As you read each verse,
you'll become more enlightened
about a key law.

It's a law that may
protect you from another's
bias in housing

or empower you
to seek justice for acts of
discrimination.

A core civil right,
fair housing is not without
its controversies.

Introduction (to provide some historical and legal background)

United States law—
federal, state, and local—
covers fair housing.

The law is robust
and protects many people
from housing bias.

Fair housing today
is nothing like it once was.
Indeed, times have changed...

First, don't forget this:
The United States began
with no fair housing.

On the contrary,
millions of people were forced
to suffer as slaves.

United States law
didn't specifically
address fair housing

until slavery
was unconstitutional
(13th Amendment).

Fair housing started
with the 1866
Civil Rights Act. Why?

To protect based on
race, color, or previous
status as a slave.

Despite a veto
(President Andrew Johnson's),
the bill became law.*

*This was just three years
after the Capitol's new
Statue of Freedom.

But so did Jim Crow, which meant discrimination was widely legal.†

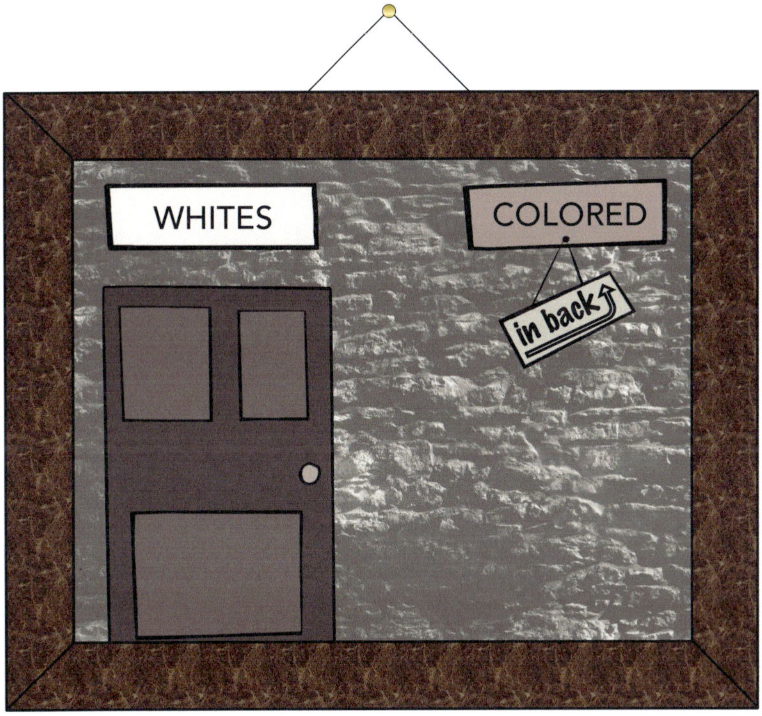

†The Supreme Court held, in *Plessy v. Ferguson* (1896), that laws promoting "separate but equal" are constitutional.

Segregation and
discrimination challenged
America's soul.

Urban riots led
to the Kerner Report, which
warned of becoming

"two societies,
one black, one white—separate
and unequal." So...

A century hence,
a new law, a different
President Johnson...

THE FAIR HOUSING ACT

PART OF THE CIVIL RIGHTS ACT,

1968

Assassination
(MLK's) led LBJ
to sign into law.

Addressing a crowd
in the White House's East Room,
LBJ proclaimed:

"The American
way of life" now embraces
"fair housing for all."

He then declared that
"the bell of freedom rings out
a little louder."

Fair Housing Basics
(How the law protects against discrimination)

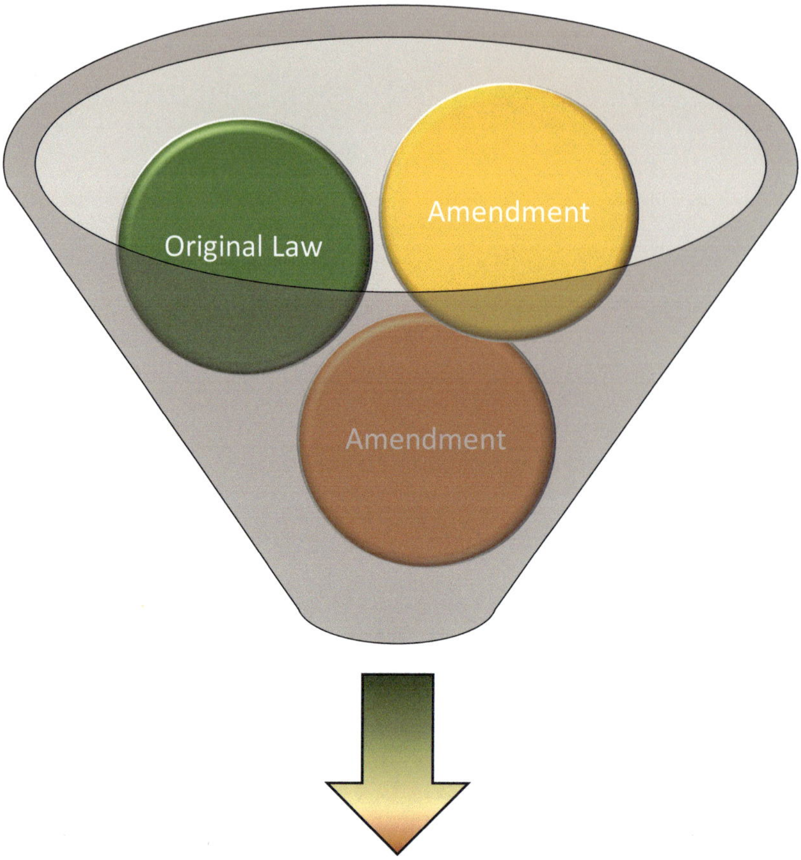

THE FAIR HOUSING ACT
(housing discrimination's
main legislation).

It was amended
and it no doubt will again
as thinking evolves.

The Fair Housing Act
applies to the whole nation
(territories too).

Coverage includes
rentals, sales, financing, and
all advertising;

luxury buildings
and affordable housing
(and all in between).*

---

*Other related laws may apply, offering additional rights.

The Americans with Disabilities Act is one example.

Exemptions include:

- ✓ buildings under five units,
  owner-occupied;

- ✓ most situations
  with single-family homes
  without a broker;

- ✓ a religious group
  limiting occupancy
  to its adherents;

- ✓ and a private club
  (similarly) preferring
  to house its members.

HUD's the enforcer;[†]
the Department of Justice
can get involved too.

[†] Housing and Urban Development is what this acronym stands for. HUD is one of the Cabinet departments—since 1965.

An "aggrieved person"
has standing to recover
under the law from

a landlord, broker,
coop board, manager, and—
you get the idea.

People who believe
they've faced discrimination
can bring a lawsuit.

Or they can pursue
an administrative route:
complaining to HUD

by phone, mail, or Web.
(There's even an app for that.)
Intake specialists

consider each case
and if HUD proceeds, then they
don't need a lawyer.

It's free and easy—
but it's still important to
proceed carefully.

The filing time frame
(statute of limitations)
depends on the route:

For federal court,
you have two years to file claims;

For HUD, only one.

An accusation
alleging housing bias
harms reputations.

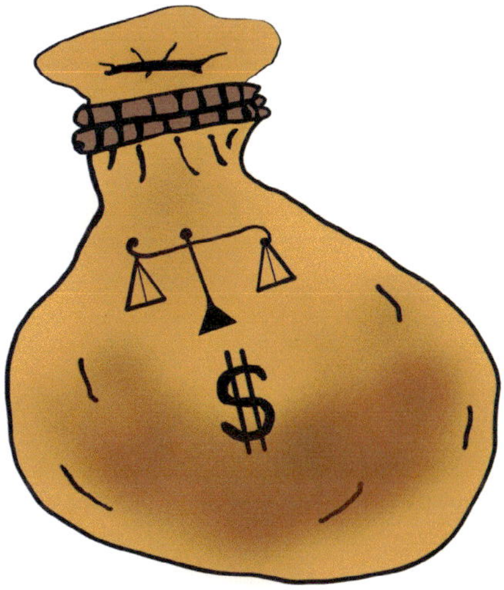

Violations bring
damages, attorney's fees,
civil penalties—

in extreme cases,
punitive damages or
even prison time.

Thousands of complaints
alleging violations
are filed every year...

But it's believed that
millions of occurrences
go unreported.

Fair housing complaints
most often concern bias
in rental housing.

is the most common basis
behind filed complaints.

Prospective tenants
can face discrimination
when seeking rentals.

Tenants have rights with

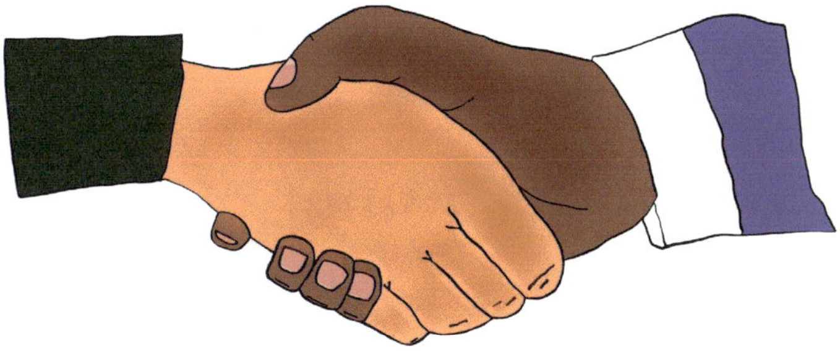

monthly rental agreements

or written leases.

Discrimination
can happen remotely, through
emails and phone calls.

Oral or written,
statements that discriminate
violate the law.

When an employee
or contractor shows bias,
landlords face risks too.

Also, a landlord
may face trouble after a
tenant complains of

harassment by a
neighbor but the landlord does
nothing in response.

Refusing to rent
based on a protected class
violates the law.

But more subtle forms
of discrimination are
also illegal.

Fair housing issues
lurk when it comes to rental
terms and conditions.

Making exceptions
or enforcing rules against
only some tenants

is illegal, if
motivated by tenants'
protected classes.

Another practice—
age-old and illegal too—
is known as "steering"...

Illegal steering:
Latinos with Latinos,
Muslims with Muslims...

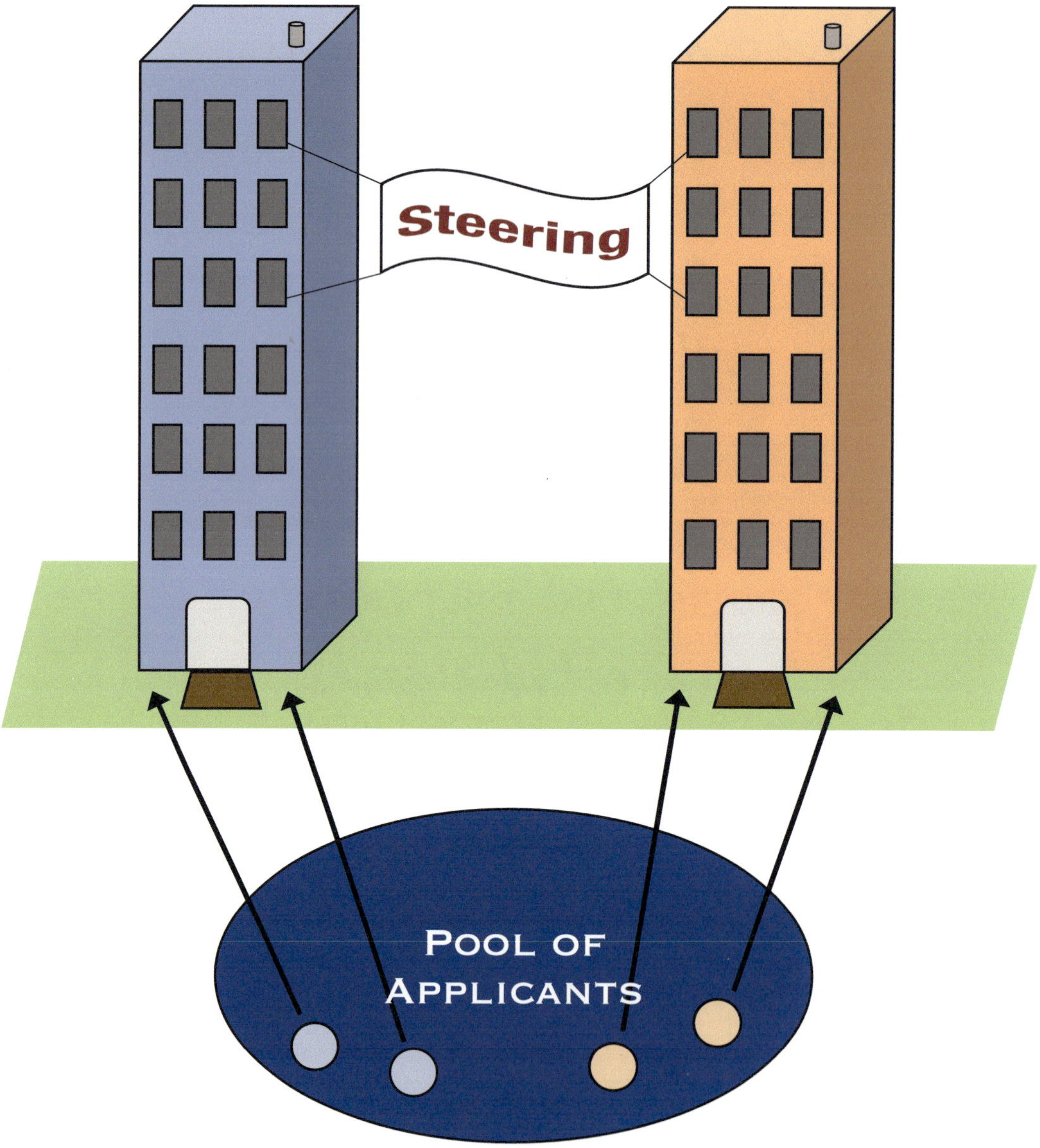

Assigning rentals
based on protected classes
is courting trouble.

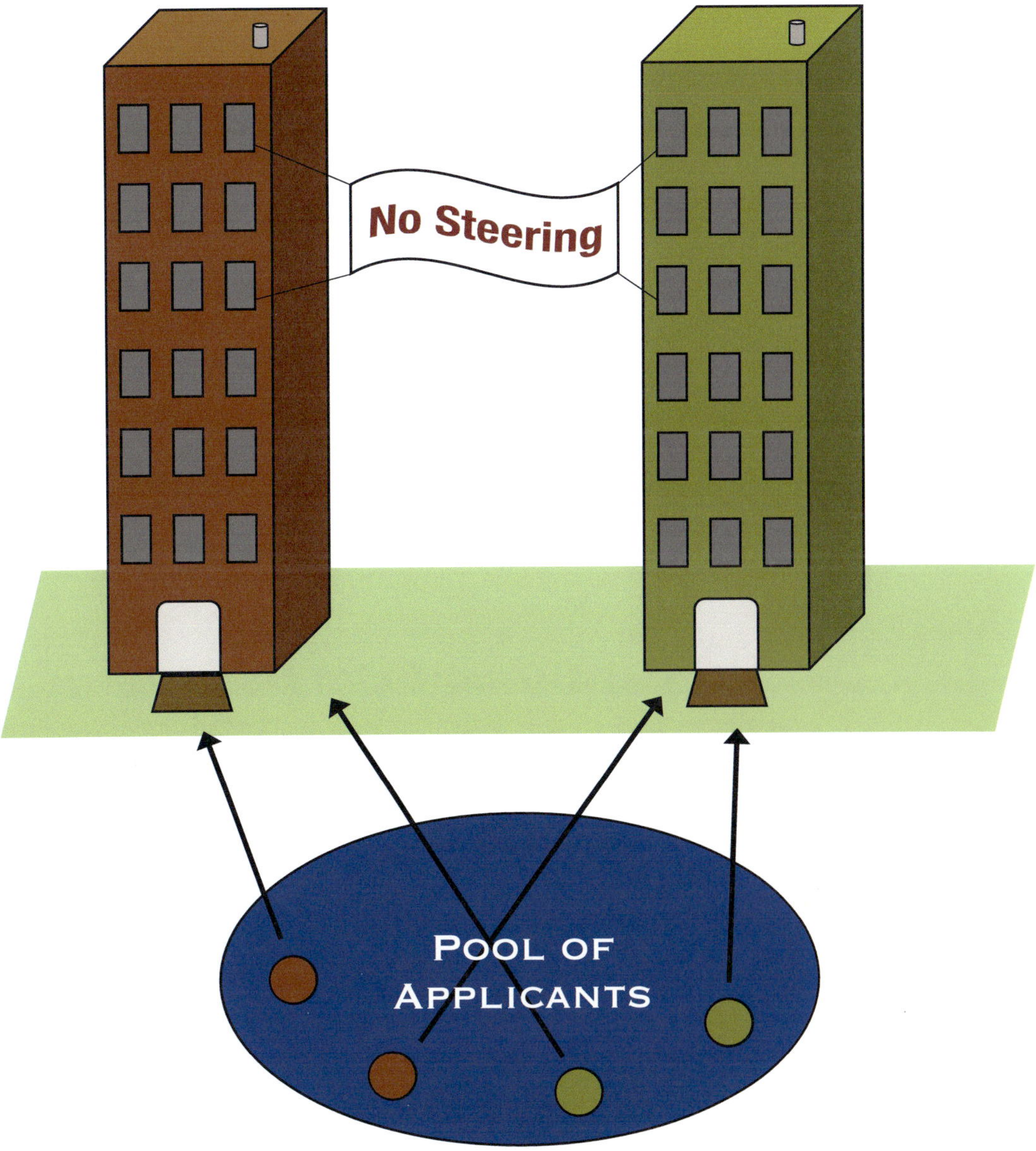

Inconsistency
can lead tenants to question
innocent mistakes...

"Any studios?"
"Yes." "Any studios?" "No."
How can both be right?

Different answers
to the very same question
can raise suspicion.

Screening applicants
to check criminal background
is fine (if not wise).

But HUD guidance says
landlords should be careful here.
Landlords should always

consider a crime's
nature, severity, and
other key factors.

The guidance also
reminds landlords to apply
screening equally.

Name and linguistic
profiling: assuming things
based just on language.

Making a judgment
or drawing conclusions when
learning a prospect's

name or when hearing
a prospect speak can lead to
unfair rejections.

Khan
Smith
Singh
Gonçalves
Taylor
Kowalski
Zhang
O'Reilly
Caruso
Hernandez
Smirnov
Haas
Levine
Jackson
Lee
Schwartz
Watanabe
Lefèvre
Yoo
Williams
Young
Nguyen
Perez

"Testing" can confirm
a prospect's allegations
of unfair treatment.

Government testers
are people who respond to
ads for apartments.

Covert but legal,
they pretend to want rentals
but check compliance.

What can testing find?
Discriminatory acts
that support a case.

EQUAL HOUSING
OPPORTUNITY

Fair housing logo—
you might see it on walls of
rental offices.

Inclusion in ads,
brochures, and such tells prospects
landlords are mindful.

No "redlining" means
lenders, insurers, brokers
can't redraw the map.

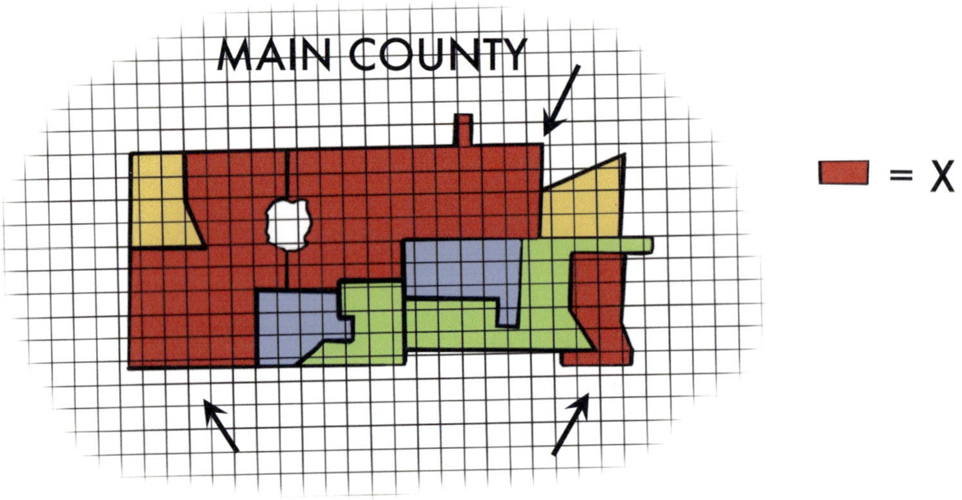

They also can't give
inferior deals based on
protected classes.

Retaliation
(when landlords punish tenants
for pursuing rights)

is illegal too—
regardless of the outcome
of the tenant's claim.

A tenant with a
losing discrimination
claim can recover

damages if some
retaliation for the
claim can be proven.

Disparate impact
(unintentional bias)
is harder to prove.

It means that a rule,
although neutrally written,
still discriminates.

"Affirmatively
further" (an old requirement)
has a new HUD rule.

It means government
needs to foster inclusion
throughout the country.

But this requirement
remains controversial; its
critics say the feds

should not engage in
such "social engineering."
The requirement was

almost axed by the
Local Zoning Decisions
Protection Act; but

the bill didn't get
to the committee stage in
the House or Senate.

Wait just a minute—
this section on basics is
getting a bit dense.

Let's now look more at
protected classes, which is
so fundamental...

Protected Classes
(Characteristics that get legal protection)

Discrimination
may be unethical, but
is it illegal?

Discrimination
based on a protected class
is what's illegal.

Protected classes
are groups of people that have
a special status.

The term refers to
characteristics that get
legal protection.

Over the decades,
protected classes have grown.
The Fair Housing Act,

which started with four,
has seen the number go up.
Now there are seven.

First came RACE, COLOR,
NATIONAL ORIGIN, plus
RELIGION, and then

amendments added
SEX, DISABILITY, and
FAMILIAL STATUS.

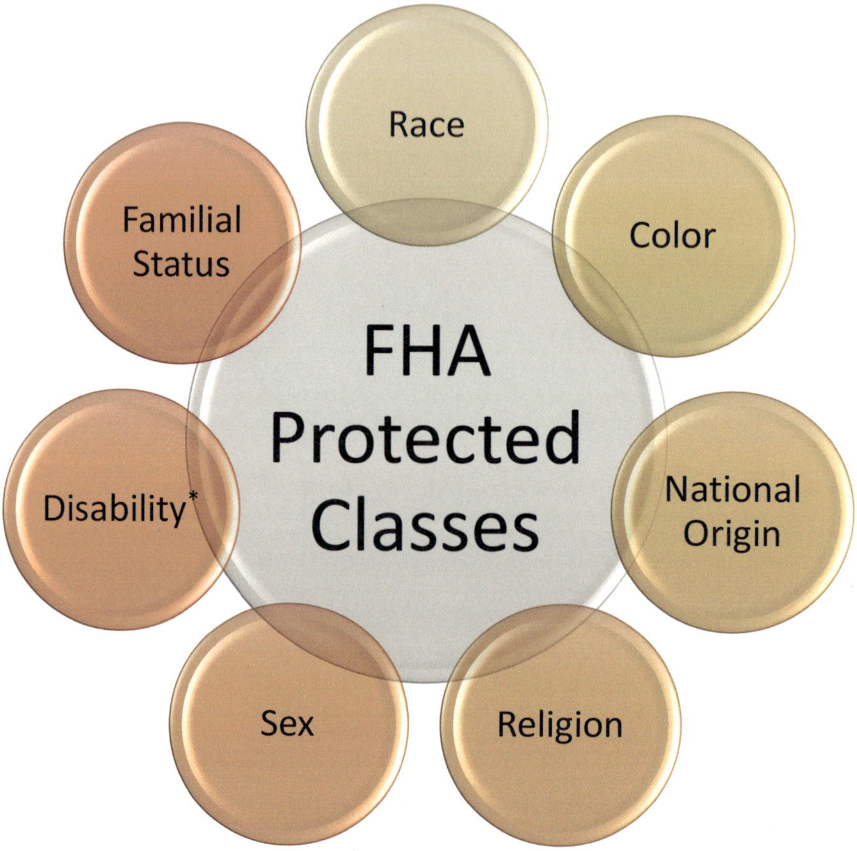

---

*"Disability"
is written as "handicap"
in the FHA.

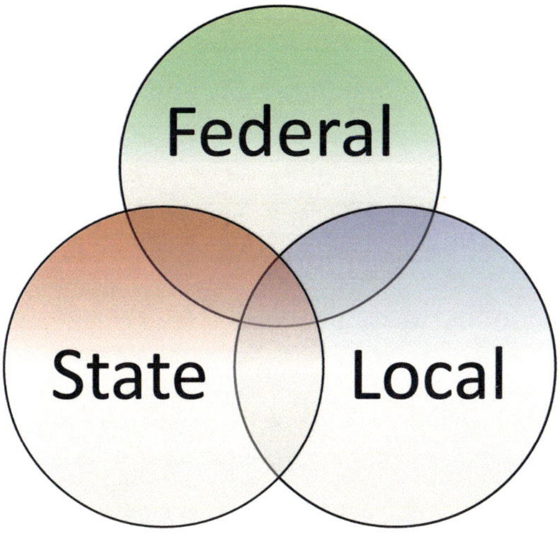

State and local laws
may include other classes;
for example, age,

marital status,
legal source of income,[†] and
gender expression.

[†]Plus, with Section 8, denying housing vouchers might be illegal if source of income is defined to encompass payments by vouchers.

Both RACE and COLOR
protect tenants whose dark skin
makes landlords say no.

WOULD YOU SAY THIS BUILDING IS MOSTLY WHITE?

ARE THERE OTHER PEOPLE LIKE ME LIVING HERE?

Conversations that concern ethnicity are big risks for landlords.

Answering questions such as these can spell trouble for any landlord.

WHAT WOULD MY NEIGHBORS LOOK LIKE?

Also, landlords can't
decide which ethnicities
won't feel quite at home.

Rejecting tenants
for this reason still equals
discrimination.

Advertisements should
display a diversity,
appealing to all.

Staff must not factor
race or color into the
decision-making.

Writing down a code
to convey a prospect's race
implies a bias.

Discrimination
by landlords against their own
race? That's not legal.

No excuse exists
for landlords who are part of
a protected class.

Scaring folks to sell
due to neighborhood changes—
It's called "blockbusting."
It gets people to
sell at low prices, fearing
that minorities
are quickly moving
into their neighborhood and
it won't be the same.

Where do you come from?
Which NATIONAL ORIGIN?
It must not matter.

Citizenship and immigration status: not in the FHA.

But screening people inconsistently (with just sporadic questions)

can lead prospects to claim national origin discrimination.

Limited English
Proficiency (LEP):
HUD warns against its

use as a pretext
for national origin
discrimination.

This protects people
who are not that fluent in
the English language.

RELIGION broadly
protects people when it comes
to expressing faith.

Observant or not,
tenants have rights regardless
of their views on God.

Holiday decor:
tenants can display or not;
it must be their choice.

Common areas
may promote holiday cheer—
but not religion.

SEX (i.e., gender)
discrimination is banned,
since '74.

Showing bias toward
women or men can lead to
new accusations.

Not just abhorrent,
sexual harassment is
outlawed by this ban.

Claims of "quid pro quo"
and "hostile environment"
are actionable.

Violence at home:
HUD guidance aims to protect
innocent victims

to help ensure they
don't get evicted just for
calling 911.

Courts are starting to
interpret sex more broadly.
Not conforming to

stereotypes with
gender is protected by
the Fair Housing Act,

a federal judge
in Colorado ruled in
Smith v. Avanti.

Related to this,
HUD's Equal Access Rule makes
sure that HUD programs

are offered without
regard to one's sexual
orientation,

marital status,
or gender identity
(effective 3/12).

Landlords can't impose
traditional gender roles
when choosing tenants.

So a single mom
can rent with her kids, just as
a single dad can.

Any maintenance,
such as shoveling the snow
or heavy yard work,

that tenants must do
while living in a rental
can't be just for men.

DISABILITY—
It can't keep tenants away
from their desired home.

Any impairment,
physical and/or mental,
that substantially

limits major life
activities meets the law's
broad definition.

HIV and AIDS:
both not public health hazards;
both get protection.

Landlords who refuse
to rent to people who have
HIV or AIDS

violate the ban
on disability-based
discrimination.

Addictions, such as
alcoholism, are all
disabilities.

But illegal use
of any controlled substance
is not protected.

When screening tenants,
landlords can reject people
with a record of

convictions for an
illegal manufacture
or distribution.

Disability,
though it's protected, cannot
excuse violence.

Dangerous tenants
who pose a threat don't merit
the law's coverage.

Landlords can't inquire
about disabilities.
(It's not their business.)

Questions about the
nature or severity
of an applicant's

disability
are not allowed under the
HUD regulations.

Landlords can't require
a prospect's assurances
of not needing help.

Not able to live
independently must not
mean no tenancy.

NO WHEELCHAIRS ← No good.
Landlords can't be so concerned
about their image.

Landlords who worry
their building will resemble
a nursing home should

fear a fair housing
complaint from prospects instead.
Wheelchairs can't be banned.

HUD has made clear that
"walk-in closets" and "great view"
are okay in ads.

(Such wording is fine
even though not everyone
can walk or see well.)

Anticipating
a tenant's special needs is
not advisable.

So many landlords,
despite some good intentions,
take fair housing risks...

Landlords who allow
assumptions to influence
housing decisions

risk being accused
of discrimination—for
limiting choices.

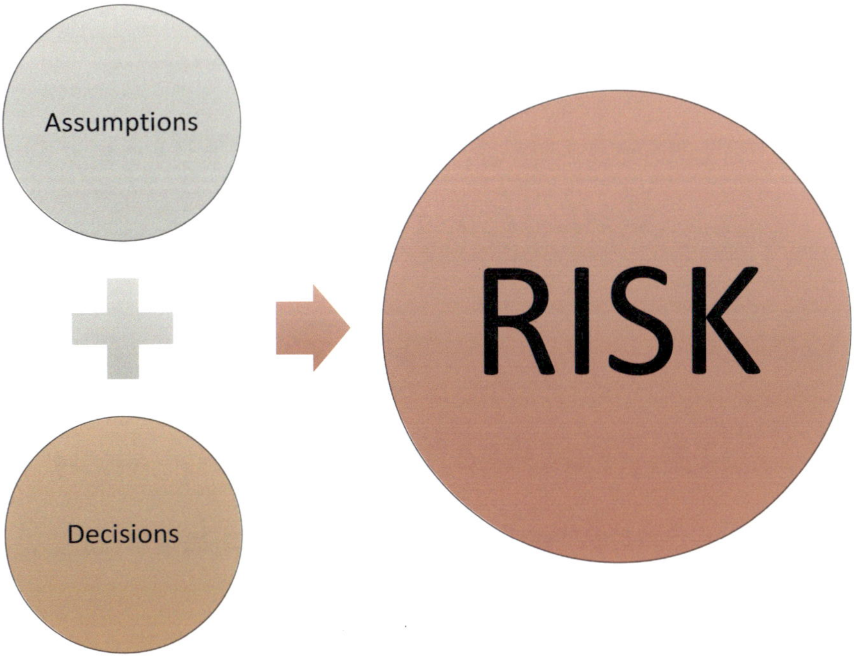

As an example,
telling prospective tenants
about vacancies

just on the ground floor
(anticipating their needs)
may seem quite helpful

if it's clear they have
mobility impairments.
But it's restrictive.

Landlords should always
let prospects bring up any
concerns they may have.

Accommodations
may be needed for tenants'
disabilities.

Examples include:

- ✓ service dog when pets are banned;
- ✓ closer parking spot;
- ✓ letting a tenant's helper use a laundry room that's meant for tenants;
- ✓ waiving a pet fee for tenants who need to keep service animals.

Undue financial,
administrative burden...
not reasonable.

If requests are for
a disability and
are reasonable,

then a landlord must
grant them. Not reasonable?
Think of more options.

Tenants can't pay for
having disabilities.
This means they cannot

be charged a higher
security deposit
or be required to

purchase insurance
because of the need for a
motorized wheelchair.

Disability
means accessibility
could be a challenge.

Building owners must
know accessibility
rules under the law.

This helps ensure that
limited mobility
is no barrier.

Landlords must approve reasonable requests for modifications.

Modifications alter a building's structure, such as WIDENED doors

or added ramps that let tenants avoid taking stairs, if difficult.

Tenants normally pay for modifications that landlords okay.

In addition, the seven design requirements might also apply...

Seven requirements
for design and construction‡
apply only to

buildings designed for
first use after 3-13-
1991.

---

‡Accessible routes,
reinforced walls for grab bars
are some examples.

Building owners may be ordered to retrofit if noncompliant.

Retrofitting means reconstructing for access—It can be pricey.

Kids are people too!
So the FHA protects
FAMILIAL STATUS.

Households with children—
at least one under 18—
are covered by law.

Parents, guardians,
even written designees
enjoy protection.

Familial status
also covers pregnancy
and all adoption.

Buildings for singles?
It would mean rejecting kids,
so that's not legal.

Rules restricting kids?
they're fine if meant to protect
health and/or safety.

Child supervision
at a playground or a pool—
a smart requirement.

Bedroom-sharing rules
risk violations based on
familial status.

Landlords who say kids
cannot room with their parents
or with their siblings

unfairly limit
families' choices, causing
them to pay more rent.

There is no excuse
for trying to help prospects
find the best rental.

So landlords must not
tell families they can't rent
because of hazards.

Nor can they suggest
other buildings because they
are more kid-friendly.

After disclosing
a lead paint hazard, it's still
up to families

to decide if they
want to live—or continue
to live—in their home.

Ads should always just describe a rental itself—not ideal tenants.

So statements such as "Perfect for empty nesters!" are problematic.

This statement implies that families with children are not as welcome.

Familial status
aims to ensure families
can find the right home.

But senior housing,
which has special requirements,
is exempt from this.

(62 and up,
and 55 and older
are the most common.)

Senior housing means
landlords can legally say,
"No children here, please."

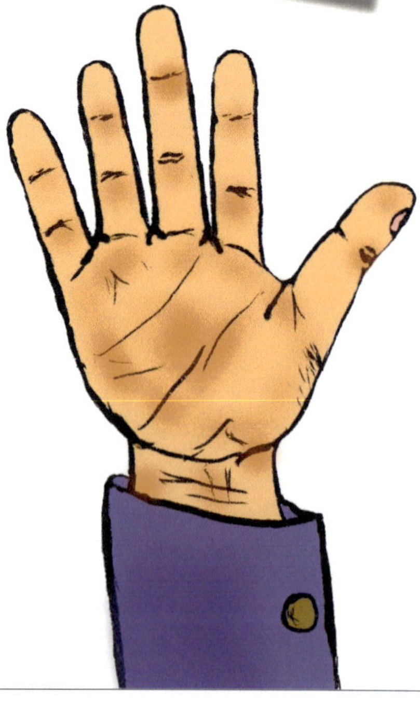

Afterword (because such a topic needs to be wrapped up properly)

Fair housing, which is
now a set of detailed laws,
started with nothing.

The laws remain a
work in progress and parts are
still controversial.

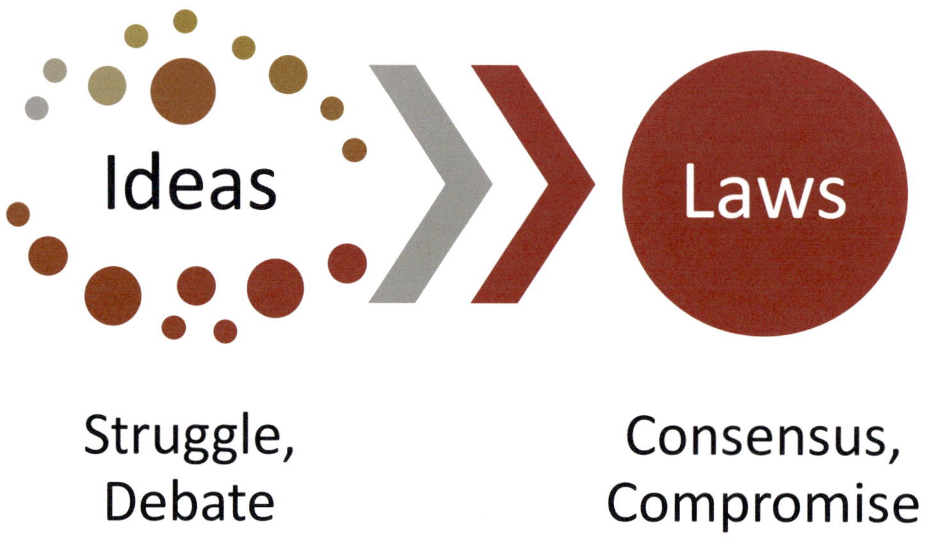

Some people contend
that fair housing goes too far.
They will argue this:

"I own property.
Why can't I just rent or sell
to people I choose?"

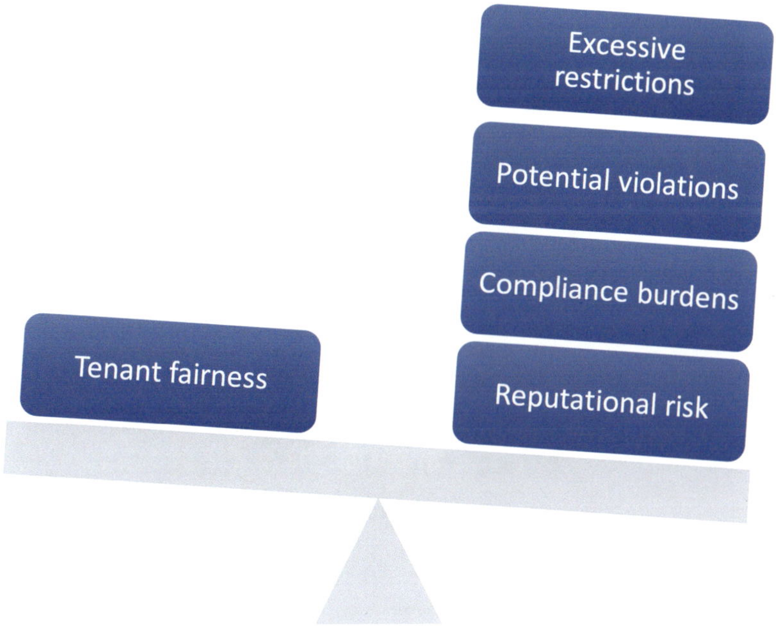

Others hail the laws,
calling them essential rules
for democracies.

They also argue
fair housing isn't just fair
but good for business.

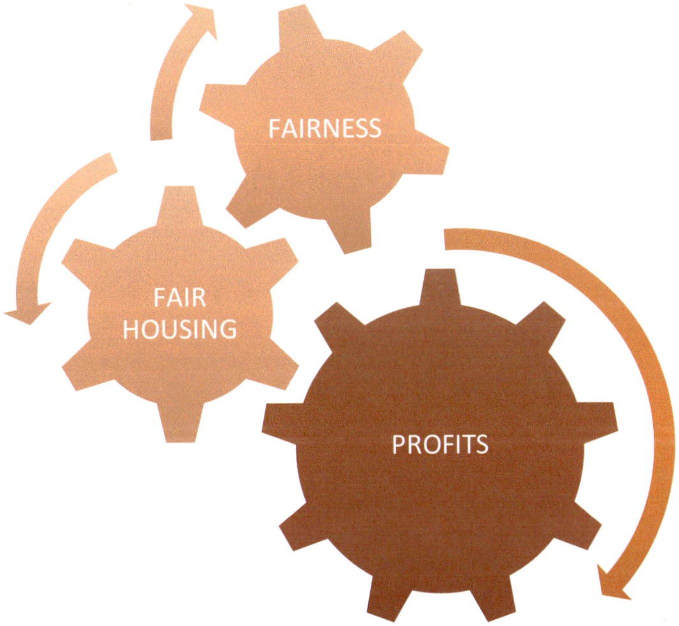

Many proponents
want more protected classes,
greater enforcement.

No matter your view,
you can express it—thanks to
the Constitution.

And so fair housing changes with the times; it's an ongoing journey.

#fairhousing50

About the Author/Illustrator

RON LESHNOWER is an attorney, fair housing trainer, and author of five books, including *Fair Housing Helper for Apartment Professionals*, which has helped many landlords achieve compliance with housing discrimination laws. A graduate of Yale University and Boston University School of Law, Ron has written extensively on government, civil rights, real estate, and the law, and he has appeared as a legal expert in media outlets such as CBS News, NBC News, and *The New York Times*.

On Twitter: @hillocrian @aboutapartments @fairhousing

For more information about this book, visit:
www.FAIRHOUSINGHAIKU.com

Made in the USA
Las Vegas, NV
07 November 2026

57673301R00069